RESEARCHING ABROAD

TIPS AND TOOLS FOR THE TRADE

D. KEITH CAMPBELL

EnerPower Press
Gonzalez, FL
2015

Cover Image: ID 44978586 © Andreykuzmin | Dreamstime.com

ISBN10: 1-63199-203-1
ISBN13: 978-1-63199-203-2

EnerPower Press
P. O. Box 841
Gonzalez, FL 32560

energion.com
pubs@energion.com
850-525-3916

TABLE OF CONTENTS

PREFACE

Before I moved to Shanghai, many wise teachers and writers sacrificially shared with me from their experiences about life abroad. "Learn the language quickly," they insightfully advised. "Immerse yourself in the culture. Find a support group. Expect and prepare for culture shock. Be patient with others. Laugh at yourself often." A particularly excellent resource full of such advice, and one that serves as a complementary companion to my work, is Michael H. Romanowski's and Teri McCarthy's, *Teaching in a Distant Classroom: Crossing Borders for Global Transformation* (IVP Books, 2009). I remain indebted to Romanowski, McCarthy, and so many others for their advice that helped me better transition to another country. However, one needed piece of advice specifically directed toward academicians serving internationally has fallen between the cracks—practical advice about how to research while living in a new and challenging environment.

Need for this advice set in quickly for me after settling into my new routine in China. After learning where to shop, meeting my colleagues, and preparing for classes, I turned my attention toward beefing up my recently completed doctoral dissertation for publication. Step one, I thought, was easy: navigate to some relevant web pages. Step two was unexpected: find out why I can't navigate to these relevant web pages! And just like that, I was introduced to the so-called "Great Firewall of China," China's pervasive, and aggravatingly intrusive, internet censorship. Days of frustration later, I discovered ways to navigate around it. This turned out to be the first of many obstacles to my research abroad.

Sometimes I navigated these new obstacles with the grace of an Olympic diver. More times than I care to confess, however, my reactions were less than stellar. On a few occasions, I'm embarrassed to say, my dilapidated, but completely innocent, desk received unwarranted blows from this frustrated abuser. Some simple tips and tools for this Visiting Lecturer of New Testament, who simply wanted to research and write while living in a distant land, would have provided some much-needed solace. And, by extension, my desk would have also breathed a deep sigh of relief! My desire to help other researchers in similar, challenging situations is why I write this brief book.

I can't take full credit for the advice that follows. After all, nothing in life is accomplished autonomously, including writing books. Many of my colleagues at Global Scholars (www.global-scholars. org), the organization I serve with, have lived and researched abroad much longer than I have. Their indirect contributions via conversations over the years weave through every page. Some of them provided input specifically related to this book. I deeply wish that I could mention all of these sacrificial scholars by name, but most serve (or, one day might serve) in undisclosed locations around the world. Simply mentioning their names in a book directed toward Christians could jeopardize their jobs and/or their well-being. I know who you are. More importantly, God knows who you are; and he will reward you accordingly. Thank you for your input! I can, however, publicly thank three wonderful colleagues: Katrina Korb, Senior Lecturer of Psychology and Education and Head of the Department of General and Applied Psychology at the University of Jos, Nigeria, offered wonderful insights from the perspective of someone who researches in Africa; Rhonda Campbell, my wife and Visiting Instructor of Oral English at Shanghai Normal University, gave invaluable input at various steps along the way; and Richard Alexander, Minister of Music and Children at Memorial Baptist Church in Norwood, North Carolina (U.S.A), kindly tweaked the final manuscript for me on a visit to Shanghai.

As you read the following tips and tools, you will quickly learn that I write as a Christian to other Christians. More specifically, for the task at hand, I write as an academic missionary to other academic missionaries, though the nature of my topic clearly makes it applicable across a wide range of religious and philosophical perspectives. (As an aside, I struggle at length with whether or not to use the term "missionary" since it is such a politically charged term in many locales around the world; I opted to retain it because most of my readers understand the term even if they would themselves prefer a different one and because it remains the simplest way to reference an important aspect of what we do). Long gone are the days when authors think that they can realistically write with a detached objectivity. Even with a topic as seemingly neutral as researching abroad, I would fool no one if I try to conceal my essential motive in writing this book: to serve God's Kingdom as a believer in Jesus Christ—the resurrected messiah, redeemer of humanity, and sovereign Lord of our universe. For this reason, I dedicate this book to Jesus, who, aside from being God's perfect missionary to humanity, commands us to love the Lord with our heart, soul, *and* mind!

INTRODUCTION:
OF MISSIONARIES AND SCHOLARS

Somewhere in the long journey of your education you heard God's call to scholarship. Maybe a professor nudged you in that direction, or perhaps it was your unquenchable thirst for knowledge. And, since you're reading this brief book, somewhere along the way God called you to serve abroad. With degree in hand, you courageously left family, friends, and security in order to serve academia in a distant classroom. Years of preparation have paid off, and now you live at the intersection of two vocational loves: mission and scholarship.

As a missionary, you're called, among other things, to travel, to learn a new culture, to speak a different language, and to eat exotic food. As a scholar—a label I use for simplicity, realizing that most of us, out of justifiable humility, would likely never attach it to ourselves—you're called, among other things, to teach, mentor students, grade papers, and direct graduate students. There is, though, one additional task that any missionary-scholar particularly struggles to fulfill: research (a term that I use in this book to collectively include, and at times use interchangeably with, writing and publishing). Research is an academic itch that all scholars live to scratch. Scratching this itch, while living in your own culture, is challenging enough. Emails. Advising students. Class preparation. And the list goes on. When you move to a locale where resources are scant, electricity is infrequent, and "turning on the air conditioning" in 100 degree weather might mean "opening the window," then advancing your field becomes exhaustingly more complicated.

It is, to say the least, much easier to write and research while working from your home country in a plush, air conditioned library than in a loud, smoke-filled office which you share with five other professors. But fret not! There is hope. In most circumstances, you can fulfill that deep longing to push your discipline forward. Helping you do this is the purpose of this book—to offer tips and tools for researching and writing while serving internationally.

I briefly mentioned a couple of these tips and tools in a 2013 article in the *Journal of The Evangelical Theological Society* (*JETS*): "The American Evangelical Academy and the World: A Challenge to Practice More Globally." My basic argument there is that, in light of America's flooded academic market, more evangelical scholars should consider practicing their disciplines abroad. Given your personal sacrifices to live missionally, this argument for you is a no-brainer. What might concern you more is a subsidiary question I ask: "Can one serve abroad and advance scholarship at the same time?" I answer "yes." But, I only offered a few passing suggestions on how to do it (e.g., use of e-books and hiring assistants), suggestions that this book builds upon.

Before adding to these comments with more tips and tools, I should clarify what qualifies me to write this book and also clarify who will most benefit from it. I have lived and researched in and around Shanghai, China for four years. During that I time, I published a monograph (*Of Heroes and Villains: The Influence of the Psalmic Lament on Synoptic Characterization*, Wipf & Stock), three peer reviewed journal articles ("The American Evangelical Academy and the World," which I mentioned above, and "New Testament Lament in Current Research and Its Implications for American Evangelicals," both in *JETS*; and "China's Intelligentsia: A Strategic Missional Opportunity" forthcoming in *Evangelical Review of Theology*), several book reviews, the book you are now reading (*Researching Abroad*), and I am currently underway with a new book for the popular press. These few publications written while living in Asia are not paradigm shifting works that will forever change my fields nor do they make me the guru of researching abroad. But, while researching and writing these works, I did pick up a number of tips and tools that seem worth passing along to you. For future editions of this book, I would love to hear by email about the tips and tools you use in your specific setting: kcampbell@global-scholars.org.

Scholars who fit into the following three categories will most benefit from this book. First, I write for those who will soon—or, who have just recently—move[d] abroad but not necessarily for those who have lived internationally for years, though seasoned academic missionaries might find a few tools to add to their own well-worn toolboxes. Since I focus on scholars who have moved from one place to another and since I frequently reference their previous home, I struggle with how to succinctly reference their previous locale. I could use the word "stateside," but some of my readers hail from Canada and beyond. "The west" sometimes proves too grammatically cumbersome, though probably all of my readers lived there. I choose, therefore, to use the word "home" in referencing your sending culture, though I am fully aware of its inadequacies; your new culture is now your home. More accurately, our home is actually nowhere in this universe; rather, our home is being prepared by Christ himself (John 14:1–4), a place where no eye has seen, no ear has heard, and no mind can understand (1 Corinthians 2:9). With this nuance in mind, please read patiently my references to your "home" culture.

Second, I focus on those serving in the world's more challenging places, where a country's general infrastructure is yet to provide stable internet, electricity, and similar amenities. Third, I direct these tips and tools to researchers who primarily serve in the arts and humanities. Others, more competent in researching the hard sciences while living abroad, will subsequently need to add more discipline-specific suggestions. With this caveat in mind, however, those researching in the hard sciences may find some of these tips and tools either directly or indirectly beneficial for their own research.

One final note: some of these tips and tools, especially those related to current technology, may prove rather elementary for my tech savvy reader. At the risk of being overly simplistic, I choose to include every applicable tip and tool that comes to mind, regardless of how obvious their implementation may seem.

TIPS FOR THE TRADE

Oscar Wilde said, "The only thing to do with good advice is to pass it on." I can't promise that all of the following advice is "good" for everyone. After all, I do agree with Sophocles: "No enemy is worse than bad advice." But, I do think that the following 24 tips, when appropriated for your own circumstances, personality, resources, and calling, will help you research and write more productively at your new address.

Tip #1: Take a Dose of Reality

All the research tips in the world do not negate your new reality; you now live in a country different than your own. Many aspects of this new life are time consuming. Learning to navigate buses, banking, and shopping takes time. Figuring out the nuances of your university and department takes time. Situating your family to another setting takes time. And, to top it off, culture shock is no fable, and it does not quickly or quietly acquiesce. Culture shock's menacing tentacles occasionally disrupt your otherwise tranquil new routine—sometimes even years after moving to your new home. This psychological nuisance steals time. To retain your sanity as it relates to your research goals—especially if your genetic cards dealt you more of a personality Type A than a Type B—you must adjust for this extra time.

Particularly in your first year abroad, therefore, suffer no shame if your productivity is not what you hope for. It is simply unrealistic to think you'll research and write as efficiently on the mission field as you did prior to it. This is a hearty dose of reality worth swallowing from the outset. However, progress can be made. And these tips of the trade will hopefully set you on the right path. Thus, you must be realistic about what you can accomplish. There is a positive side, however. Although the output may be less, the quality may increase since the very result of living internationally can add new insights to your work (something I discuss below).

Another dose of reality is the financial expense of researching and writing productively while living internationally. Some of the following tips can be expensive. A few of you—from the more lucrative fields—rake in substantial bling for teaching. Most of us don't. In fact, many of you likely receive (at least partially) the sacrificial support of faithful donors. If you want to research abroad, budget for it in advance.

TIP #2 : SLAY THE DRAGON OF GUILT

You've prepared your whole life to serve in your new culture with untold hours in classrooms, in front of computers composing research papers, fulfilling teaching assignments, and attending conferences. All augmented with herculean stamina in part-time jobs and, most likely, with a stellar spouse rooting for you at every juncture. The money invested in these endeavors might make Bill Gates raise a brow (upon further thought, probably not … but it is still expensive). And, to top it off, people and Churches back home probably funnel money into your ministry.

Cast on this backdrop, when the dust settles from your move, a voice from within may whisper, "What a waste of resources to spend X number of hours per week hunched over a desk with book in hand and computer powered on when there are so many students and colleagues to reach." On one level, I empathize with this sentiment; we do move abroad to teach and to build relationships. And, we should, indeed, invest a lot of time in them. However, a call to scholarship is a call to research. And, research requires time at a desk. Therefore, a call to university service should not devolve into guilt over time spent on research.

More importantly, there's a deeper issue related to philosophically polarizing research and ministry, as if they are at odds with one another. Simply put, phrasing it in such a polarizing way is a false dichotomy. Research is ministering to people—it is just delayed ministering to people. Let me explain. When I teach in the classroom or meet with students, I influence lives instantaneously. I speak words, and at that moment people change, whether slightly or significantly. Research, on the other hand, ministers to, and changes, people in the distant future, when the quality of your teaching gradually increases or when the research is finally published and read by students and colleagues.   Furthermore, good research opens doors. It fosters respect in the academy, thus providing platforms that you otherwise might not have, including opportunities to give more lectures, teach certain classes, and to more easily relocate when the time arises. It also fosters respect with your peers, opening doors to share your faith because they likely value research themselves. In short, good scholarship for a professor represents a good testimony both to other scholars and to your institution. Equally important, Paul tells us, "Whatever you do, work at it with all your heart, as working for the Lord" (Colossians 3:23).

It's one thing for you, personally, to understand that research and ministry are two sides of the same philosophical coin, but it is another thing altogether for some donors back home to accept it. Perhaps you have donors who view ministry as something like this: "If it ain't preaching, it ain't ministry." I understand the sentiment. There is no getting around the fact that New Testament Christianity is directly linked with verbally sharing the Gospel. Scripture expects obedient Christians—scholars included—to actively engage unbelievers. But, do keep in mind that Paul, a man who thought Jesus could return at any moment (1 Thessalonians 4:15–18) and a man whose missional fervor led him voluntarily to an early grave (Acts 21:13), took the time to research and to write theological masterpieces (e.g., Romans). Research, then, is ministry well worth pursuing. Waste no time, therefore, in slaying the dragon of guilt when he illogically proposes to dichotomize research and ministry.

Donors can grow in their own understanding of ministry through well-rounded updates of your work. Alongside your tales from afar about culture, evangelism, family, and new friends, occasionally keep them abreast of your research and the impact it has. When appropriate, communicate to them that the Bible supports a life of the mind (e.g., the very nature of Paul's writings assumes scholarly reflection as defined by ancient standards [see also Matthew 22:37]), and relate to them that they benefit from research more than they might realize. For example, almost every fact in a reputable Study Bible or commentary cost someone years (and, in many cases, decades) of research. As donors gradually learn these important lessons, then your guilt about spending your time researching will diminish. More importantly, your donors will grow to respect and value such an exceptionally influential ministry.

Tip #3: Tame the Ticking Clock: Negotiate in Advance

Clocks tick at the same pace whether you live in New York or Nepal. However, there are often more things—and certainly more unexpected things—to fit into every hour while living internationally, where routine errands like buying groceries can take twice as long. Resources abound in the West with advice on how researchers should manage the ticking clock: be disciplined, avoid procrastination, write regularly, schedule your writing, know your rhythm (are you a morning or evening writer?), take care of yourself physically (exercise, eat properly, take breaks, get enough sleep), just get started even if what you are writing is not yet good enough, eliminate distractions, secure deadlines because they can be motivating, and, finally, read good books about writing such as those by Paul Sylvia, *How to Write A Lot: A Practical Guide to Academic Writing* (American Psychological Association, 2007) and Howard S. Becker, *Writing for Social Scientists: How to Start and Finish Your Thesis, Book, or Article* (University of Chicago Press, 2007). I do not replicate their good advice here but only mention tips specifically pertinent to living overseas. Since taming the clock often proves most challenging, I give substantial space to it in the next seven tips.

Taming the clock can begin before you ever arrive on campus. In many international universities, faculty and staff are insanely overworked, and the amount of bureaucratic red tape is simply astounding. Deans and presidents frequently call last-minute meetings, and they fully expect their professors to be there, even if they had other plans for weeks in advance. You may arrive in a setting where superiors assume for you similar expectations. You can begin navigating this, if possible and if appropriate, by negotiating in advance for research time.

Understanding such negotiations relative to your new culture is imperative. Contracts and negotiations can mean something different for you than they do for your new colleagues. You might arrive on campus thinking that you and your superiors are on the same page because of what appears to you as a clearly written contract, when actually you might not even be in the same book! Because cultures are so diverse, I am unable to offer specific tips on navigating these interchanges. A good resource to begin with is Scott Moreau's, Evvy Campbell's, and Susan Greener's new book, *Effective Intercultural Communication: A Christian Perspective* (Baker Academic, 2014). My general advice here is, after arriving at your new post, to gently remind your superiors in culturally sensitive ways of your agreements about research. Ask your new, national colleagues how to do this effectively and sensitively, and remember that this may require a delicate touch. On the one hand, you need time to research. On the other hand, you don't want to inadvertently play the role of the dictatorial foreigner demanding his or her hegemonic ways.

Negotiating for this time will mutually benefit both you and the institution. For you, obviously, it affords time to pursue an important part of your academic calling. For the institution, it reinforces the fact that time spent on research can benefit their own university. It enhances pedagogy and increases professor morale. Furthermore, it encourages university personnel to think long term. For example, it might challenge them to incrementally come to understand that the financial benefits of each professor teaching twelve classes per semester are short-lived because, over the long haul, quality decreases.

TIP #4: TAME THE TICKING CLOCK: DON'T REINVENT THE WHEEL

With a reality check in place, unnecessary guilt addressed, and negotiations sought in advance, undergird all the advice that follows with this tip: ask your new local colleagues how they go about their research and how they navigate the administrative structures of their institution. It would, after all, be presumptuous at worst and a comical oversight at best to ask how to research abroad and never explore answers with nationals who have already done it for years. Find out from them how your new institution regards research, rewards it, encourages it, and interprets it.

Tip #5: Tame the Ticking Clock: Find the Right Place and Time

With your superiors (hopefully) on board and with advice in hand from your new colleagues, finding an actual place to research can prove especially challenging, even if your institution provides an office. Your office may be noisy, crowded, prone to interruptions, filled with cigarette smoke, and perhaps has no access to clean restrooms! Part of your negotiations may include time away from the office for research. Your new house or apartment may be the best location. However, your new residence may be too small, especially if you have a family. As with many aspects of your new life, you will need to be creative. Maybe there is a quiet and remote place in the library, a vacant room somewhere on campus, or a restaurant or coffee shop down the street. If affordable in your city, routine stays at a local hotel could offer you the tranquility needed to push your work forward. If forced to research in a loud office or at a small desk relegated to the corner of a heavily-traveled bedroom, then consider investing in noise canceling headphones. Or, simply drown out excessive noise through your cellphone earbuds (discussed further below).

Closely related to finding the right place is finding the right time to research. Different cultures have different routines. In some locales, you can easily research in the evenings after supper. In other locales, you might need to wake up early to make it work. Many Nigerian scholars, so I am told, take a weekend or a week off at a retreat center, away from phone, family, work, and other interruptions, to write intensively.

Tip #6: Tame the Ticking Clock: Back up Your Data

In many cultural contexts, viruses, thieving, and electricity-fried electronics are much more frequent than back home. I suggest some tools in the next section for backing up your data. Here, I need only to mention that you should have a plan in place for lost information.

Tip #7: Tame the Ticking Clock: Recruit Help from Locals

Most of these first several tips about taming the ticking clock cost little more than your time and ingenuity. The next two tips cost money, but they may be worth it, depending on your particular situation and budget. You might consider employing help from two types of locals. First, hire one or more student assistants. Back home, universities and seminaries frequently provide graders. Usually, this is not the case abroad. But, you can hire your own graders, and even expand their responsibilities to include running errands, showing you quicker ways to do things, and helping you navigate language barriers. Additionally, if you have a particularly competent student or two, then you can hire them to help you research and write. Most students will excitedly jump at the opportunity to work with you a few hours a week. Beyond freeing up some of your time, this also allows you to invest more deeply in one or two students, and, to their benefit, it adds experience to their developing résumé and helps them pay for their tuition and their travels to and from school. For those that more specifically help you research and write, you will especially invest in the next generation of scholars.

Second, employ a house cleaner. Investing in someone to clean is, at least for me, internally conflicting, as it can smack of elitism. After all, as so many people (perhaps justifiably) assume, only the über-wealthy pay others to clean for them. This is precisely, for good reason, what you do not want your donors to think. For this reason, among others, my wife and I have not hired a house cleaner in China. If we had three toddlers traipsing around Shanghai with us, then we might reconsider! The fact is, however, that there are usually significant differences between hiring a cleaner in your new locale and in hiring one back home. For one, house cleaners back home are generally quite expensive while, in most places abroad, they are very affordable. Additionally, the time it takes to accomplish routine things in your new culture, especially with kids, increases significantly. Hiring a house cleaner in most countries is not only an affordable time-saver, but it often provides a good job for a needy person. Equally important, this person frequently grows close to your family, thus providing ministry opportunities otherwise not afforded.

TIP #8: TAME THE TICKING CLOCK: TRAVEL WISELY

Another potentially expensive tip that helps save time is to use "research friendly" means of travel. If you live where frequent travel is necessary, then strategically choosing how you travel will give you hours of extra time to accomplish certain tasks. Take Shanghai, for example. You can travel locally by foot, bicycle, electric bicycle, bus, subway, or taxi. Faster and more convenient means of travel, such as taxis, cost more money. Although taxis are an expensive mode of travel, it provides the best setting to read, check emails, return texts, and plan meetings. Thus, at times it may be wiser to spend an hour sitting in a taxi with laptop open than standing in a crowded subway.

TIP #9: TAMING THE TICKING CLOCK: RELEARN "YES" AND "NO"

You have likely learned appropriate ways in your native language to politely say "yes" or "no" to a colleague's invitation or suggestion. You may need to relearn this skill at your new university because saying "yes" and "no" is not as simple in some cultures as simply saying "yes" and "no"! My monocultural friends may balk at this, because it seems like a terribly absurd suggestion. Expats who live in Asia, however, will respond with an understanding nod. In an attempt to "save and give face," my Chinese friends and colleagues, for example, will often avoid directly saying "no," though both parties in the conversation are expected to understand clearly that "no" has been communicated.

Knowledge of this simple fact would have saved me a lot of confusion a few years ago in an email exchange with a Vietnamese professor who had invited me to present a paper at a conference in Ho Chi Minh City. He politely asked me to change the title of my paper, "Science Emerging in China with Religion-Like Characteristics." He wanted me to replace the word "China" with "Asia." The professor did not tell me something that I learned much later from another source, that he was trying to avoid losing face with his colleagues because of my specific—possibly negative—mention of China. Relative to my American, academic culture, I humbly challenged his suggestion that I change my title, and, though honestly open to changing it, I provided solid reasons to keep "China" in my title. The most important reason for me to retain "China" was that my knowledge of the rest of Asia was simply too limited.

Instead of my rhetoric communicating to him, "I am open to what you're saying, but let's discuss this more," it, instead, communicated, "No! I am not going to change the title of my paper." I failed to know this! As a result, he told me: "No, you cannot present that paper at our conference." But, the way he communicated this "no" was lost on me at the time: he invited me to present the paper at a conference later that year, when, he explained, it would be better received. To me, he was not saying "no," but "wait." So, I was thrilled to get to travel, albeit later, to Vietnam to present my paper! I learned subsequently, however, that there was really no conference later that year! In his mind, he was not ambiguous; he clearly communicated "no." Case closed. Why did he communicate "no" in such an indirect way? He did not want me, a fellow professor, to lose face because of rejection. He was actually being polite. But, I thought he really wanted me to present my paper at another time. Knowing this would have prevented the string of embarrassingly awkward emails that followed!

The world's cultures are too diverse and too complex for me to offer specific advice about how to say "yes" and "no" in every context. My tip here is simple: through whatever means—conversations with expats and locals, reading books about the culture, and/or inquiring from Google—learn how to say "yes" and "no" and then apply it appropriately with your colleagues to free up more time for research.

TIP #10: TAME THE TICKING CLOCK: A CAVEAT AND SOME PERSPECTIVE

Before wrapping things up about taming the ticking clock, allow me to make an important caveat and provide some perspective. First, a caveat. Managing time to allow for research abroad requires a delicate balance. Part of the reason for serving internationally is to practice missional hospitality to students and colleagues (Christopher J. Freet, *A New Look at Hospitality as a Key to Missions*, Energion Publications, 2014) and to immerse yourself in a new culture, while refusing to hermit away in an office every day. You don't want to withdraw from the very culture that you're there to learn and serve.

Striking this balance depends a lot on your own personality. My more extroverted colleagues frequently leave their office doors open and beckon students to drop in unexpectedly and never seem to experience decreasing academic output because of it. In fact, they draw energy from it. My more introverted colleagues, conversely, still love to meet with students but usually need advanced notice in order to psychologically prepare for the encounter so as not to deplete their emotional resources. If America is your home culture and if you find yourself leaning more toward the introversion side of the continuum, then perhaps you have felt pressure to feel guilty about your regulated isolation. Don't fall prey, however, to the arbitrarily imposed assumption that extroversion is some type of objective ideal (see Susan Cain, *Quiet: The Power of Introverts in a World that Can't Stop Talking*, Broadway Books, 2013). Most of the world's population, namely in Asia, are more introverted than extroverted. Jesus, too, often sought isolation (John 6:15).

Also, a word about perspective, especially for my more "Type A" colleagues. I have been discussing how to "Tame the Ticking Clock." This phrase has Western sentiments dripping from every corner. Keep in mind that you might serve in a culture where "the clock" does not mean the same as it does for you. For many, the clock ranks dozens of rungs down the ladder of importance, behind things like "saving face" or "talking about the weather." Adjusting to a different set of expectations about time, especially for Type A personalities, can be a beautiful exercise in spiritual formation. Perhaps a healthy perspective is to follow the advice I received from a friend who teaches in an undisclosed location in Africa: "Ideally, you want to conform your standards and routines as much as possible to those of your national colleagues. Find out what everyone else does when the lights go out. If they just sit and chat with neighbors, then maybe you should do the same thing too!"

With this caveat, this perspective, and these time saving tips in place, when your scheduled research time arrives—*and this is important*—use that time for research!

Tip #11: Order an Extra Dose of Patience

Although you do everything possible to tame the clock, it will still be more frustratingly challenging at times than back in your home country. If you move to China, for example, it will likely take weeks to iron out the wrinkles of navigating internet censorship (see discussion below about VPNs). Or, if you move to Nigeria, adjusting to intermittent electricity and employee strikes will cause frustration. There will likely come a time, after the internet fails or the electricity goes out, when you drop your head and, with blood pressure rising, threaten to give up all hope of any productive research. Don't throw your computer through the window! Be patient with yourself (Galatians 5:22). Be patient with your new environment. In time, you will find more productive means to accomplish your research.

Tip #12: Tap into a Well of Encouragement and Motivation

As your patience decreases, your encouragement and motivation may decline with it. As time consuming endeavors that are so simple to accomplish back home continue to crowd out research, a longing to toss in the towel may become appealing. Adding insult to injury, your university or department may not value research as much as you do. Or, worse, they may never even think about it. Although with time and discipline you might acquire the patience of Job, you may still on occasion become discouraged and unmotivated. When this happens, remember your calling. If you are called to research, then God will provide the time to do it. Ask for help from your spouse and family to hold you accountable to stick to it. Or, find a research accountability partner either back home or in your new culture. And, be encouraged knowing that, as leading missiologist Timothy Tennent once quipped, the Apostle Paul was simultaneously one of the world's greatest missionaries and at the same time one of the world's greatest theologians. Few researchers have contributed more than Paul to the advancement of a particular field. Be encouraged! You can concomitantly research and be a missionary.

Tip #13: Plan Ahead for Unexpected Down Time

Regardless of how much you plan ahead and no matter how patient you are, inevitably life abroad will deal you a healthy dose of unwanted downtime. Right in the middle of writing an article, the electricity will go out or the internet will crash; en route to your favorite café for some scheduled writing, a traffic jam will leave you for two hours in the backseat of a cab; or, a student protest will provide you an unexpected holiday. Appropriating some of the right tools that I discuss in the next section will keep you researching during such interruptions. At this point, suffice it to say: be prepared for it! For example, if electricity is unreliable, then always have hard copies of materials on hand so that you can continue working. If you travel on unpredictable roads, even for short trips to the grocery store, or if you live in a culture where meetings rarely begin on time, then always carry along work materials. Be prepared in advance to work offline in the following ways: compose outgoing emails in your favorite word processor and save them to send later (or use Gmail Offline or a similar platform that I discuss in the next section); cut and paste important emails into a word processor for convenient viewing; and transfer articles, blogs, and websites to some of the apps discussed below.

There is another challenge particularly relevant for the academic missionary that often leads to unwanted downtime. Somewhere amidst the smooth sailing of your research, you will come across a much needed book or article that is snugly nestled in a library somewhere on the other side of Planet Earth. Back home, remedying this problem was easy; simply walk across the courtyard to the library and check it out, make copies, or order it through inter-library loan. When in The Gambia, however, this can bring your research to a grinding halt because only someone from home can get it for you. The next four tips offer some practical advice on navigating this specific challenge. Here, I simply suggest to be prepared for it. One way to prepare is to work on several projects at once, including the writing of popular pieces that require fewer resources (like the book you are currently reading!). When a hard-to-get resource is frustratingly out of reach, then set into motion the process of retrieving it by using the next several tips and, while you wait, move on to another project.

Tip #14: Hire an Assistant from Your Home Country

I can hardly overstate the help provided by an assistant from home. This is likely one of the most important tips I offer, and every researcher living abroad should consider it. Here are three things to know about hiring an assitant from home. First, you need to decide who to hire. The best assistants from home are undergraduate or (preferably) graduate students who live on or near a campus with a library that fits your needs. These students often look for part time, flexible work with low demands to augment their other employment. Related to this, consider hiring two assistants (one that you promise a certain number of hours weekly and another one who works as needed) so that if one quits unexpectedly or is unable to perform a certain task, then your research can continue unhindered.

Second, decide what types of things that they can do for you. They can scan and email you articles and portions of books that cannot be accessed abroad. Especially helpful is that most university and seminary libraries today provide free scanning. They can edit your newsletters and build bibliographies for you. Depending on their ability, they can even edit and write for you. The number of hours per week or month can be as flexible as your needs. I have hired assistants to work on an as-needed basis, while others have worked 5 hours per month and at 10 hours per week. Finally, you will need to advertise for an assistant. The easiest way is to post an advertisement for the position on campus bulletin boards and/ or at campus websites. If you do not live near the campus, usually you can find a professor, staff member, or a colleague who will sympathize with your mission and be glad to help. Simply email them your job description and have them post it for you. An easy way to hire subsequent assistants is, once the first one moves on, to ask him or her to recommend any friends who might be interested in working for you.

Hiring an assistant benefits not only your research, but it also benefits the employee and (perhaps) your new, national colleagues in several influential ways. It often provides a mentoring relationship between you and your assistants. It gives them opportunity to work internationally, exposing them to other cultures. Also, it can increase their interest in missions. And, occasionally, if you have the money to pay them for extra hours, you might ask your assistants to help a local, national scholar obtain resources for a project.

Tip #15: Utilize Volunteers from Your Home Country

A few strategic volunteers can complement your paid assistants. In most circumstances, volunteers cannot replace paid assistants because paid assistants live on, or next to a campus, and their job is to react quickly to your requests. But, volunteers can save you money, for example, by ordering a needed book and mailing it to you, by running errands, or by making a few needed phone calls. If you are blessed to have volunteers who live near a library, then they can take on some of your assistants' responsibilities, further saving you money.

Tip #16: Get to Know a Librarian

An ideal volunteer is a librarian (or a library employee) who sympathizes with your calling. He or she can help you obtain sources that few others can. He or she need not work at a world class library, although that would be best. Remember, modern inter-library loan systems are fabulous. So, a community college librarian may prove more helpful than first meets the eye.

Tip #17: Email an Author

Occasionally, you might need an article that you or your assistant simply can't find. Or, you may be faced with buying an expensive monograph, just for a chapter or two from it. In such cases, consider contacting the author directly to ask for a PDF of the article or a specific section of the monograph. Often, if you explain your situation, including the sacrifices you're making to serve internationally where national scholars are not afforded the luxury to do what Western scholars so freely and easily do, they are often eager, and honored, to help.

The same applies for conference papers. Often the expense and time involved in traveling to conferences are too high for you to attend. However, if you see advertised a presentation that might benefit your research, a brief perusal of the internet often turns up an email address for the presenter. In my experience, presenters are usually flattered that I am interested in their work and are eager to help scholars in our situation by passing along their papers and notes.

Your situation may differ, but I have never had a professor turn me down after I explain my situation. On one occasion, I needed a German book that my assistant and I simply could not find. I contacted the author in Germany, and he kindly and quickly mailed me a copy by snail mail, all the way to China!

Tip #18: Collaborate with Colleagues Back Home

Collaborating with peers is wise regardless of where you live. It provides accountability, better perspective, and it cuts the workload in half. Collaborating with scholars back home has some added benefits. They can, for example, help you obtain resources and keep you abreast of quickly changing academic fields. Furthermore, your new life abroad, as mentioned above and as discussed more fully below, will likely benefit your research projects because of the fresh perspectives your international experience brings to the table.

Tip #19: Collaborate with Colleagues in your New Culture

Collaboration with colleagues in your new culture can also ease some of the burdens of researching abroad. The benefits are generally the same as collaborating with colleagues back home, but with some added challenges and benefits. Challenges include the following. First, differing perspectives on time and deadlines may cause misunderstandings. Second, if you plan to publish your results in English and if English is your colleague's second language, then you will likely bear extra editing responsibilities. Conversely, if you plan to publish your results in your new host language and if you are not conversant in it, then you will ultimately have to trust your colleague's translation. Finally, there are often unstated but assumed differences of social power that can lead to miscommunication and misunderstandings; in other words, your colleague may see you as "more powerful" simply because you are a foreigner, and thus communicate with you differently (e.g., afraid to say "no" directly) (see Moreau, et al, *Effective Intercultural Communication*, chapter 12). On most occasions, you can overcome these challenges by assuming a proper posture of humility—by "considering [your national colleague] as better than yourself" (Philippians 2:3).

The benefits of collaborating with your new colleagues, however, probably outweigh the challenges. Working with a colleague who understands the local academy can help with a host of things. They are better connected in your new country than you are, more intricately understand local needs, can better research locally, and can translate work into local languages if needed. Aside from helping you do better research, collaborating with a national colleague will help you be a better researcher. As a missionary, you well know the benefits of working with people from other countries (e.g., exposure to new perspectives on life); research is no different.

Finally, beyond benefiting you and your research, collaborating with a colleague can benefit them for all of the same reasons it benefits you. But, there may be extra benefits for them. In low-income countries, resources are often hard to find; by collaborating with you, nationals will have access to resources that they otherwise could never use. Closely related to this, collaborating with nationals, especially those who cannot access good resources, will help develop their research skills.

TIP #20: BE CAREFUL WITH INFORMED CONSENT

If your research requires interviews with locals, then know that informed consent procedures can be tricky, because nationals may not understand exactly what it means. Given the dangers often involved for people in many countries, it is always best to err on the side of caution when using real names. For example, careless journalists recently published the names of Boko Haram victims in Nigeria, which placed them in grave danger. If you doubt whether your interviewee understands the informed consent process, then strongly consider using a pseudonym.

TIP #21: CONSCIOUSLY FOLLOW ETHICAL GUIDELINES

In some settings, research methods might be unethical, but they are practiced for the sake of convenience. Examples might include plagiarism, ill treatment of others, bribery, and fees for publishing. As Christ's representatives, we need to set the pace for what is ethically appropriate with our research, resisting the urge to take short cuts at the expense of our integrity and at the expense of others. The challenge, of course, is that navigating ethical conundrums in your new culture will not always be black-and-white. Take, for instance, publication fees for journals which are usually scorned in the West but are mandatory in Nigeria where there are no rich publishing companies to subsidize the efforts. It is beyond the scope of this book—and well beyond my expertise—to offer an ethical rubric for your research abroad. My best advice is to learn the particular nuances of your new host culture, be immersed in Scripture, have at least a working knowledge of the discipline of ethics in general and of ethics relative to your new context, and, finally, expect on occasion to have your sense of morality challenged.

Tip #22: Learn to Love E-Reading

A decade or so ago pundits often debated the future of e-books. "Will e-books displace traditional hardbacks," they pondered? "Will libraries go the way of dinosaurs? Will e-books be around in 50 years?" Although I cannot predict the place of hardbacks and libraries in the lives of tomorrow's bibliophiles, I confidently predict that e-reading is here to stay. Amazon's ultimate goal, for example, is to make its entire 1.8 million volume library accessible in e-book format. All readers, but especially academic missionaries, will benefit from transitioning, at least in part, to electronic devices. My colleague who serves in an undisclosed location in Africa offered this quip in a personal correspondence about researching abroad: "You can't even get off the ground without [an e-reader]!" I evaluate in my next section the current electronic devices on the market. Here, I simply mention the benefits of learning to love e-reading.

Some of my readers in their 20s and early 30s, with a scratch of the head, may wonder who in the modern west does not read materials in e-format? But people from my generation (the middle-aged crowd) sometimes struggle to adjust to reading and researching on a digital device. The feel of a book in their hand is simply too natural, easy, and irresistible. "Flipping through the pages" of an e-book is awkward and cumbersome. I resonate! At 40 years old, I never read my first e-book until my mid-thirties. Five years later, believe it or not, I prefer e-books to hardbacks. My notes and highlights are searchable, buying books on the go via the web is simple, traveling with a hundred pdf files is no problem, navigating my book is easy, switching between books is a breeze, looking up words in a dictionary is a tap away, enlarging font for ailing eyes takes only one click, and I can quit reading on page 78 on my iPad and pick up my iPhone and continue reading on page 78!

I must admit, the transition is difficult, but it is doable. Throughout my undergrad, graduate, and PhD studies, I never once read an e-book. The mission field forced me to use them. And, I am glad it did. The academic payoff is worth it, not to mention the freedom it provides while traveling is priceless. So, bite the bullet, begin building your electronic library, dive into an e-book or two, and learn to love them.

Tip #23: You Still Need Hardback Books

Although you now adore e-books more than ever, you will still need the occasional hardback because many books—especially academic ones—are not yet available in e-format and because in most cases you cannot share or loan e-books to colleagues. You can get needed hardback books by planning ahead in several ways. First, simply bring them with you on your flights. Since weight dictates price when checking bags on all airlines, bring books in your carry-on luggage. Second, if colleagues, friends, or friends of friends are traveling through, then ask them to bring books for you. Third, have someone mail them to you. Be careful with this last suggestion, however. Not only is it expensive, but given the varying quality of postal services around the world, your books may never arrive. Finally, if all else fails and if copyright laws permit, have your assistant or volunteer scan the entire book and email it to you. If copyright laws do not permit scanning books, then contact the publisher, explain your situation, ask them for a PDF copy of the book, and offer to pay for it.

Tip #24: Where to Publish

After you have slain the dragon of guilt, tamed the ticking clock, increased your patience, navigated downtime, hired assistants, rounded up some volunteers back home, strategized with colleagues, taken care with informed consent, learned to love e-reading, and, with a large helping of God's wonderful grace, proven to yourself that you can research and write abroad, it is now time to submit your work for publication. But where?

If possible—that is, if there are publishing venues available—you should try to advance scholarship in your new host country by writing papers, articles, textbooks, monographs, etc. Or, at least you will likely want to find creative ways to disseminate scholarship from abroad in your new setting. If publishing venues are not available, then you may want to initiate one or two such venues in cooperation with competent national scholars. When publishing locally, you need to consult more intentionally with national colleagues because you may need to avoid many subtle, unspoken expectations (like unstated submission guidelines or politically sensitive words).

You probably already aspire to these kinds of goals because they reside so deeply at the heart of what we do as academic missionaries. But, should you spend your limited time trying to publish in what are generally flooded markets back home, thus taking time away from your service abroad? The answer probably depends on your discipline. Perhaps your field is internationalized enough to make the point moot; that is, it is irrelevant where you publish your research because all of your new, international colleagues and students will read it anyway. However, the case may differ if, for example, your field is theology because a theologian in Africa has the option to publish in several reputable African Journals that largely (and unfortunately) go unread and uncited in the West.

If you do have a choice where to publish, then how exactly do you choose? Ultimately, only you can prayerfully adjudicate that decision based on your gifts, opportunities, goals, and interests. With that said, perhaps a both/and, rather than an either/or, approach is better. Publishing in your new culture is advantageous for what I trust are obvious reasons. Back home, it is quite likely that colleagues need scholarship from those who have lived at length in other cultures and, as a result, have gained new insights into their respective disciplines. A specific example of cross-cultural experience that advanced a particular discipline that I mention in my article, "The American Evangelical Academy and the World," is the work of Timothy Laniak, Professor of Old Testament and Academic Dean at Gordon-Conwell Theological Seminary in Charlotte, N.C:

> [Laniak says that] living with Bedouin in Israel and Egypt helped inform his biblical theology of leadership, *Shepherds After My Own Heart: Pastoral Traditions and Leadership in the Bible* [Downers Grove: InterVarsity, 2006, p.13]. [He] elsewhere confirms how serving at length internationally gave him insights into Scripture that he otherwise would never have had: "Listening to Christian leaders in other parts of the world constantly challenged my interpretation of Scripture" ["My Journey: A Personal Word from Tim Laniak" <http://shepherd-leader.com/about.php>, accessed April 12, 2015].

Aside from the mutual benefits that your previous and new culture will gain from this both/and approach, it will, hopefully, help ameliorate the unhealthy tendency toward western academic hegemony.

TOOLS FOR THE TRADE

All researchers need tools for the work they do—books, computers, journals, etc. While living abroad you need these tools and more. Specifically, you need ones best suited for international life where travel-difficulties, power outages, and daily nuisances are the norm. Mentioning every tool available to any given researcher is impossible and unnecessary. Here I only mention tools most helpful for academic missionaries. I should emphasize again what I have highlighted numerous times above: none of these tools provide the convenience of a cozy, predictable, office back home. But using the following tools, the ones that fit your particular budget and situation, can make your research abroad go as smoothly as possible.

TOOL #1: ELECTRONIC DEVICES: THE iPAD

The iPad. Expensive? Yes. Quite helpful? Without a doubt. Why so helpful? Because it provides a research platform beyond your computer that, in my experience, no other digital device provides. The iPad has its drawbacks: extensive typing is cumbersome (unless you purchase a keyboard; see below), there are no backspace or tab keys, and, as just mentioned, it is pricey. The pros, however, far outweigh the cons. Think of the iPad as a multifunctional tool comparable to a Swiss Army Knife. First, it gives you more mobility with your research than does a computer. It is much easier and quicker, for example, to use an iPad instead of a laptop on a crowded bus or in a taxi; I am, for example, typing these words on a cramped, Shanghai bus. Second, the iPad will keep your research going when your electricity goes out, or if your computer crashes or is stolen. Finally, it is the best e-reader on the market with every major bookseller represented in Apple's app market, thus allowing you to travel with an extensive library.

I suggest investing in the standard size iPad instead of the iPad Mini because the screen on the standard size gives you the feel of reading a normal-sized book instead of reading only partial pages. This proves especially helpful when reading PDFs. Additionally, I suggest investing in a good iPad case since you will likely travel in rugged places. I certainly do not recommend Apple's iPad case. It is too flimsy, cheaply made, and it does not sturdily hold the iPad upright.

Tool #2: Electronic Devices: Other Tablets

To save money, you may be tempted to rely solely on a Kindle Fire or some other similarly affordable tablet. With all things equal, a cheaper tablet may serve your needs fine. But, all things are not equal. You need the best tablet for research while living abroad. The size and functionality of the iPad make it the best option for this. Falling for the temptation to save money on cheaper tablets will result in only frustration and hindered research.

Now that I have sufficiently hailed the iPad as a superb tool for researching in your new host country, and in an attempt to avoid propagating an unnecessary tech-elitism, let me say a few words about other tablets. E-ink e-readers may serve as a nice supplement for the iPad, especially for users who live in countries that experience extended power outages. In layman's terms, an e-ink e-reader is a digital device that lets you store and read books, the pages of which resemble traditionally printed pages (with black-and-white type) instead of a computer screen. Excluded from these devices are the bells and whistles of beautifully-displayed colored pages, apps, and music. Although you can connect to Wi-Fi with these devices, web-surfing is practically impossible because their wireless connectivity is primarily designed for purchasing books.

However, the benefits of e-ink e-readers are twofold. First, and most importantly, these devices frequently have nearly a one month battery life! Contrast with the iPad that will only last a full day with light usage. The e-ink e-reader's long battery life proves especially helpful for those experiencing extended power outages. Secondly, these devices are a good choice for those who read outside, because the iPad is virtually useless in direct sunlight or bright light.

The best e-ink e-reader on the market for researchers is the very affordable Kindle by Amazon. There are several varieties (e.g., "Kindle Paperwhite" and "Kindle Keyboard") that basically do the same things but have different features. The Kindle is better than, say, the Nook because of Amazon's superior selection of e-books. Aside from purchasing and reading books, the Kindle lets you download and read PDFs, syncs nicely with the iPad, and many have 3G capabilities. Do not confuse Kindle e-ink e-readers with the Kindle Fire, another product from Amazon. The Kindle Fire is similar in appearance and function to an iPad, the size of which is between the regular iPad and the iPad Mini. If you own an iPad, the Kindle Fire is unnecessary because the iPad will do everything the Kindle Fire can do and much, much more.

TOOL #3: ELECTRONIC DEVICES: iPHONE

Like the Kindle, the iPhone supplements the iPad. I specifically recommend the iPhone over other phones because, if you accept my advice about the iPad and Kindle, then the iPhone is your most logical choice in cell phones because it syncs so smoothly with the other devices. The iPhone's size and accessibility are precisely its advantage for quick reading, studying, and reviewing in crowded busses, subways, and supermarkets. Whereas you have to dig into a backpack or briefcase to retrieve an iPad or Kindle, the iPhone snaps easily onto your belt, drops in a purse, or slides into a back pocket.

The best use of the iPhone, because of its size, is not so much for reading articles or books while traveling around town, though you can use it in that way within limits. Rather, it is best used to study and review things that can more easily be done while riding in a cab for 20 minutes. What kinds of things do I have in mind? Most likely you will have to study a new language (or stay fresh with research languages) when you move abroad. Myriads of language acquisition apps are available that provide the perfect platform for brief intermittent study while skipping through town, thus eliminating antiquated and cumbersome flashcards. Or, to offer other examples, with the iPhone you can review class notes, meeting agendas, and brainstorm ideas while in quick transit. The 20 minutes used during these brief forays of study or review equates to 20 minutes of office time that you can reallocate for more detailed research.

Tool #4: Computer with no Handheld Devices

My love for handheld devices and my biased bent toward their utility for research surfaces clearly in the previous three tools (iPad, other tablets, and iPhone), and you may get the impression that it is impossible to research abroad without them or without the current apps that they offer (discussed below). Now permit me to make a qualification: you are not doomed to an academically unproductive stay in your host culture without these tools. In many cases, they simply streamline your research, especially if you travel. They make reading e-documents and e-books easier than a computer, and they provide alternatives for remaining productive during power outages. However, my colleague who teaches in an undisclosed location in Southeast Asia related to me, "I have none of these [devices], yet...I have become more productive in [my new country of service] than I ever was in the United States. So [research] is still possible for those of us in laptop land." Hopefully this is good news if you are on a restricted budget.

If you do stay in laptop land, then few things electronically will likely change about how you conduct your research, though you may want to consider some of the programs mentioned next.

Tool #5: Apps and Computer Programs

Owning the right devices is one thing. Maximizing their use for research while abroad is another thing. The market is saturated with apps; and computer programs will specifically help maximize your research efforts, either by directly making researching abroad easier or by indirectly freeing up more time to use for research. Mentioning every available app and program is, of course, impossible. Rather, I can only mention here a representative sampling. Although I mention most apps and programs by company name, remember that, nearly always, competitors who offer similar products might better meet your specific needs. So, I encourage you to see my suggestions more as a general guide than as a prescribed trek. I only discuss here apps and programs that will generally appeal to researchers more broadly and do not discuss field-specific apps or programs (e.g., Logos Bible for Bible researchers). Finally, I do not discuss websites (such as the wonderfully helpful Google Books) because there are simply too many to address, and I assume you already know what sites are most apropos for your specific discipline.

A = App only
AC = App and Computer program

The Amazon app and website is primarily intended to help you shop at amazon.com, but it is also useful for research. Many of their books are searchable, and most include a table of contents.

Calibre (AC) is a free e-book library management program that offers the following features: library management, e-book conversion, syncing of all e-book reader devices, conversion of pdf's into e-book formats, and downloading news from the web and converting it into e-book form.

Clear (A) is an exceptionally intuitive, elegant, and free to-do list that syncs across all Mac products.

Docusign Ink (A) lets you sign documents from abroad.

Dropbox (AC) works as a folder on your desktop that stores your documents online so that you can access them from other devices while on the go. It is ideal for sharing and editing documents with others and for backing up your data.

EndNote and *Zotero* (C) are reference management software packages used to manage bibliographies and references when writing articles, essays, dissertations, books, and monographs.

Evernote (AC) is a wonderful platform to make notes (including audio and video), compile research, brainstorm, edit pdf's, and collect web articles. These documents are then accessible across all devices and can be shared with others. A downside to the free version of Evernote is that you must be online to use it.

Gmail Offline (AC) is a Google Chrome app that lets you read and manage messages when you don't have an internet connection and then automatically sends the messages when you reconnect to the internet. Compare with similar features available with Mozilla Thunderbird and Microsoft Outlook.

Googledocs (AC) is a word processor that functions much like Microsoft Word except it is entirely cloud based, allowing instant, remote backup. Similar to Dropbox it allows you to share and edit documents with others, and it has optional password protection.

iBooks (AC) is Apple's e-book app that is similar to the Kindle App and comes already installed on your Apple devices, but its book-selection is smaller than that found at amazon.com.

Kindle App (AC), already alluded to above, syncs all your reading material across devices and turns your iPad or iPhone into an elegant e-reader for books, textbooks, PDFs, newspapers, magazines, and more. It also provides, at your fingertips, the vast resources available for purchase at amazon.com.

Myriads of language apps (both for your target language and for research languages) will keep you studying while on-the-go.

LogMeIn (AC) is a handy app that syncs your iPad to your laptop or home computer so that you can access your computer from your iPad. In other words, you can leave your computer at home, and, when logged into LogMeIn, your computer screen will appear on your iPad, allowing you access to folders, documents, and everything else on your computer. Its primary weakness is that both your iPad and computer must be online, making it impractical for some users while traveling. Originally, LogMeIn offered this app for free. Now it costs about $70.

Microsoft Office (AC) now offers their line of products in Apple's App Store, albeit with an expensive yearly price tag of about $100. This permits better interfacing between the iPad and PC products, including Word, Excel, and PowerPoint.

Mozy (AC) is an online, data backup service for both Windows and Mac users. It backs up your data automatically in your computer's background so that if an electrical surge fries your motherboard, then you can easily access all of your documents, pictures, and movies from another computer or device. Since Mozy runs in the background, you don't have to remember to back up your computer. In the event your computer crashes, is stolen, or is otherwise inaccessible, Mozy will save you weeks of time and headaches.

Notability (A) is helpful for those who like to "handwrite" notes instead of type them. It lets you easily "write" directly on your iPad screen with either your finger or a stylus (purchased separately online or available at most office supply stores). These notes are then easily edited (including the helpful function of cutting and pasting your own handwritten notes), stored, saved as PDFs, and/or emailed to yourself or others. A unique function of Notability is that it ingeniously lets you write with large handwriting that then is simultaneously transferred into a smaller text, which allows you to fit more words to a digital page.

Pages (AC) is Apple's free, and exceptionally user-friendly, word processor that functions similarly to Word in Microsoft Office. It interfaces well with Word documents (though expect a few minor glitches), pdf's, and other platforms. Documents in Pages sync across your devices, including PCs.

PDF Expert (A) is an exceptionally helpful app that lets you open and annotate pdf's, allowing you to make highlights and take notes on the pdf document itself. Compare with Adobe Acrobat.

Pocket (AC) lets you save websites for later viewing (both while online and offline), which conveniently permits you to catch up on blogs and online articles and reviews during power outages and while on airplanes, trains, and buses. Note that Evernote recently added a similar feature to its product line.

Prayer Notes (A) helps organize your prayer requests and keep track with when and how God answers them.

Rosetta Stone (AC) is a fabulous, though quite expensive, language acquisition tool. It is not the Holy Grail of language products as its advertisers tout. But, it is a wonderful tool to complement your language study. It is especially helpful for vocabulary and syntactical acquisition and retention.

SimplyNoise (A) provides background noise via earphones for those who struggle to concentrate in loud places.

Siri (factory installed on all newer iPhones and iPads) is Apple's, sometimes witty, digital personal assistant and knowledge navigator. Siri is software that allows you to talk with your device. "She" does things like respond to your questions by searching the internet for answers, by making appointments for you, or by looking up a contact. Most beneficial for the international researcher is Siri's voice-recognition software that allows you to dictate emails, notes, and word documents. Instead of typing responses to incessant emails that flood your inbox, simply speak your reply. Instead of typing a paragraph of your research, just speak it. Siri is good (actually, she is awesome!), but she is not perfect. She requires an internet connection, which may prove intermittently problematic in some settings. And, dictating technical aspects of an article will likely prove too difficult for her. Furthermore, she sometimes struggles to understand certain accents, like Bostonians who omit their "r's" or American Southerners who transform monosyllable words into multi-syllable words. In general, however, her accuracy makes composing many documents much easier than hand typing them. Thus, in spite of her weaknesses, Siri is well worth getting to know, as she can save valuable time, especially when plodding through emails and articles.

T&TMPD (AC) and *Donor Manager* (A; AC forthcoming) are among a number of free donor manager programs that help save time in organizing and communicating with donors. T&TMPD is sophisticated and contains extensive bells-and-whistles. The downside to T&TMPD is that it almost does too much and can be complicated and cumbersome to use. Donor Manager, on the other hand, is extremely user friendly, but it cannot perform some of the sophisticated tasks that T&TMPD can do. For example, Donor Manager's search function is, at times, too simplistic.

TurboScan (A) turns your iPhone and iPad into a portable scanner. It is useful for scanning receipts for reimbursements, for capturing journal articles in a local library, or for generally reducing paper clutter.

A *VPN* (Virtual Private Network) (AC), which provides both a secure internet connection and access to blocked websites, is necessary in many countries where internet censorship is enforced. 12VPN and Strong VPN are two excellent choices (between $75 and $100 yearly). Some countries like China will occasionally temporarily block VPNs. These internet crackdowns can be painfully aggravating. In such circumstances, buying two VPNs may prove to be a wise investment. I do not suggest using free VPNs in internet-censored countries because they do not provide the customer-support that you will likely need from time-to-time.

TOOL #6: INTERNET

Pay the highest price for fastest internet service available. Consider, as an additional service where available, adding 3G or 4G wireless to your iPhone or iPad for travel and for power outages. Remember that you can create a hotspot from your iPhone or iPad to provide wireless internet to other devices.

TOOL #7: TRAVEL ACCESSORIES

Whether flying across the ocean or buzzing around town, these few travel accessories will complement your research while on the go.

A six foot drop cord helps you connect to receptacles in restaurants, classrooms, or airports that are just beyond reach of your computer's charger.

A multiple outlet plug solves the frustrating problem of successfully finding a receptacle to charge your dead iPad only to see that two travelers beat you to it. With a multiple outlet plug in hand, you politely interrupt them, ask if you can share the outlet, divide the electrical current via your multiple outlet plug, insert your six foot drop cord, move to your own space a few feet away, and return to writing your article.

For those who find it difficult to type at length on the iPad, perhaps a bluetooth keyboard is worth the investment. I particularly like Logitech's "Keys-to-Go" because it is small, rugged, easily packable, and has an astounding three month battery life. One potential drawback is that it does not come with an iPad stand.

External Battery Pack for charging cell phones, tablets, and other devices (except laptops and computers; see next entry). I suggest the RavPower 15,000mAh Deluxe Portable Charger with iSmart Technology (3rd Generation) (about $40), which will recharge an iPhone 5s seven times or an iPad one time.

Extended-life batteries for computers are helpful in locales where electrical outages are the norm or if you frequently travel long distances.

CONCLUSION: BE ENCOURAGED

As you step out in faith to live the life-of-the-mind in another country, be encouraged! Although you will leave a lot behind—family, friends, safety, and comfort—you do not have to leave behind your love for advancing your field. In other words, heeding God's call to academic missions does not have to halt your research. Rather, it can enhance it. With the right tips and tools, you can live out both of your vocational loves, mission and research. Although the advice offered in this book will not guarantee smooth sailing in the rough waters of academic missions, these tips and tools—along with those that you learn on your own—will add a refreshing and much needed breeze to your academic sails.

www.ingramcontent.com/pod-product-compliance
Lightning Source LLC
Chambersburg PA
CBHW021120020426

42331CB00004B/566